CW00504381

Freedom

from the

Learn 22 activities to reduce or stop the persistent,
incessant, constant, obsessive, compulsive, racing,
ceaseless babble of the mind

GET FREEDOM FROM THE EVER CHATTERING, RESTLESS MIND

VISHAL GUPTA

FREEDOM FROM THE MONKEY MIND

Copyright @ Vishal Gupta. All Rights Reserved

First Edition 2021

Authors Name: Vishal Gupta

ISBN :

Published by : Self Published

Publishers address :
Flat no 31-A, Miramar Building,
Napeansea Road,
Next to St. Stephens Church,
Mumbai 400026.

OTHER BOOKS BY THE AUTHOR

Crying Baby Watching Hen

THE MIND
IS LIKE A MONKEY,
WHICH IS DRUNK, BITTEN BY
A SCORPION AND POSSESSED BY
A GHOST. LEARN TO TRAIN IT
AND TAME IT.

UNLEASH THE
INFINITE POTENTIAL OF
YOUR MIND. NEVER EVER
SUFFER FROM ANY
MENTAL BLOCKS.

VISHAL GUPTA

#1 Bestseller in Multiple Categories
https://vishal-gupta.com/CBWH-kindle-universalworld

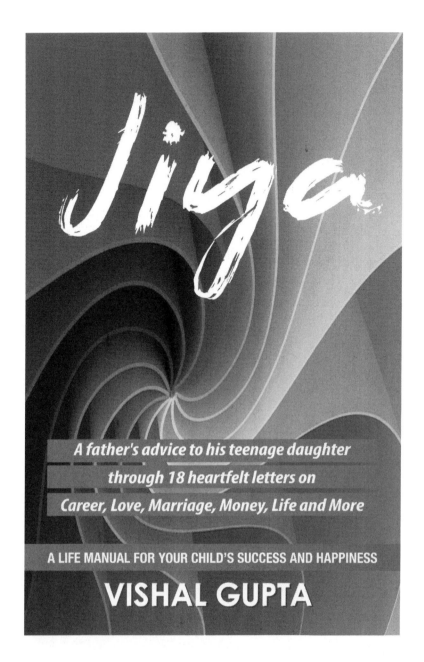

Jiya

A father's advice to his teenage daughter
through 18 heartfelt letters on
Career, Love, Marriage, Money, Life and More

A LIFE MANUAL FOR YOUR CHILD'S SUCCESS AND HAPPINESS

VISHAL GUPTA

#1 Bestseller in Multiple Categories
https://vishal-gupta.com/jiya-relink-universal-link

kefi

A Single Idea
From This
Book Can Change
Your Life.
If I Can Be Happy,
So Can You !

25 Things I do Every Day to Keep Myself Happy, Joyful and Enthusiastic, Every Second, Every Day, ALWAYS

VISHAL GUPTA

#1 Bestseller in Multiple Categories
https://vishal-gupta.com/kefi

ATARAXIA

21 PLACES TO VISIT
FOR COMPLETE LIFE TRANSFORMATION

Human Life is a Privilege. Don't Waste it. Visit the 21 Places Mentioned in this Book to get a First Hand Experience of Life and Transform your Life Forever.

VISHAL GUPTA

#1 Bestseller in Multiple Categories
https://vishal-gupta.com/ataraxia

HIGH ON LIFE

ARE YOU

DEPRESSED
STRESSED
UNHAPPY
NERVOUS
ANXIOUS
PANICKY?

A Personal Account of How I Beat Depression of 7 years.
20 Powerful Activities to Uplift your Mood Instantaneously. Never feel
Depressed Again. Invest in your Mental Health. Do not live in Denial.

THERE IS NOBODY MORE IMPORTANT THAN YOU!

VISHAL GUPTA

#1 Bestseller in Multiple Categories
https://vishal-gupta.com/high-on-life

Learn to WIN ARGUMENTS and SUCCEED

20 powerful techniques to never lose an argument again, with real-life examples. A life skill for everyone.

Best Seller
★★★★★
Multiple Categories

VISHAL GUPTA

#1 Bestseller in Multiple Categories
https://vishal-gupta.com/win-arguments-succeed

I am honored and excited to know that you have purchased this book and invested your hard-earned money and given your precious time.

As an act of appreciation and gratitude, I would like to offer you a FREE GIFT:

Click below to download a free copy of my book "TOXIC PEOPLE."

This book has transformed the lives of thousands worldwide, and I am sure it will also be helpful to you.

So, what are you waiting for?

GRAB YOUR FREE COPY BY CLICKING ON THE LINK BELOW:

http://vishal-gupta.com/freebook

What is this book about?

This book discusses 22 activities that will give **immediate temporary relief** to a person from the **chatter, babble, and control** of our restless, obsessive, neurotic mind.

Though the relief will be temporary, it will be effective. It will give a person a **short time window** to **break away** from the phobic stream of vicious thoughts that are disturbing and controlling that person, and it will allow that person to take back control of their mind.

I'm sure most readers may have experienced that when we are **under the grip** of our negative or depressive thoughts, we can't seem to break away from that thought process leading us to more of those destructive streams of vicious thinking. The 22 techniques given in this book will allow a person a **small gap where** they can divert their thought flow to something more productive and positive.

Most of us **completely identify with our minds**. What this means is that we think that we are our minds. However, the opposite is true. **We are not our minds**. We are our pure conscious awareness, and the mind is a **different entity**. But we are so identified with our thoughts(mind) that we do not experience this difference.

There are two types of awareness (only for the sake of understanding this discussion).

The first type is our **waking awareness,** in which we do our daily chores like eating, talking, working, and moving. This type of awareness is not our true awareness. In this type of awareness, we **live our lives 100 percent through our minds**. Our minds rule over us. We act per the whims and fancies of our mind, satisfying its every desire and being under its complete control. We have no freedom from our minds. We become its slave.

The second type is our **true and pure awareness**. This true awareness is that **watcher** inside us that is watching and observing everything that we do 24 × 7 × 365. It is watching us at all possible times, including during sleep and deep sleep. This watcher never leaves us and is our **true essence**. This watcher is formless, infinite, and dimensionless. People call this watcher by many names. Some of the common names are:

Universal energy, God, Omnipresent, Omnipotent, Omniscience, the Eternal, the Highest Truth, the soul, presence, the isness, our true being, ultimate reality, and more.

This pure awareness is not an object. We **cannot see it or touch it**. However, we can experience it and **'BE'** it.

With this type of awareness, we live our lives with **the intelligence of this universal energy,** devoid of the control of our minds. The more aware we become of our pure awareness, the less we live out of our minds and the more freedom we have from them.

Therefore, we either live through our minds or live through our pure awareness.

When we live through our minds, we feel out of control, tensed, stressed and like a puppet. We have no control over the mischief and nuisance of our minds. The mind behaves like a **dictator king, and we become its slave**.

In contrast, when we live our lives through our **awareness**, we become the **king** and use our mind as an assistant to help us accomplish whatever we want.

This book is about 22 techniques and activities that use **different characteristics** and qualities of the mind to **manipulate it and influence** it in such a manner that the mind is forced to stop or reduce its control over us.

Each technique will give us an opportunity to break the chain from *living through our mind to living through our awareness*.

This book is about getting freedom from the clutches of our monkey minds.

Who should read this book?

Millions of people are suffering due to their monkey minds.

Obsessive thinking, negative thinking, and **overthinking** have become diseases.

It is now unanimously agreed by doctors that the **untamed** and **uncontrolled** mind has become the number one **killer,** beating all other diseases hands down. The mind, which was once **gifted by God** to humans as a tool and an assistant to do great things for the progress of the species, has **sabotaged** us and taken over. The mind that was once an obedient servant has overthrown us from our thrones; it has become the king, and we are its slaves.

This book is for those people who want to get their thrones back. It is for those people who want to get liberty from the **clutches** and grip of a tyrant king. It is for those who want their lives back and are fed up with dancing to the tune of the mind.

It is for people who want freedom from their monkey minds!

How to read this book?

This book can either **save** your life or **change** your life for the better.

Do not read this book like a novel. Enjoy this book as a **connoisseur** tastes wine. **Go slow.** Don't be in a hurry to complete the book. Your goal should **not** be to browse the book and become more intellectual. Your goal should be to understand the intricacies and **nuances** of the mind and become its **master**.

Look at this book to learn about the **characteristics** and functioning of your mind. Follow it to be able to manage your monkey mind **lifelong**. If you can **imbibe** and implement the teachings of this book, you will be able to experience joy and bliss throughout the journey of your life.

Read it to **tame and train** the monkey mind!

Authors note

This book is an outcome of my struggle with *depression and obsessive-compulsive and hyper nature.* Having **suffered** for many years and then successfully **winning** over them, I have made it my **life mission** to spread **my knowledge** and experience on how to tame, train, and control the mind. Today, as I write this book, I have gained complete freedom from my earlier **hyper, compulsive, and restless** mind. I remember that phase as a faint memory in time. I no longer suffer from the chaotic, incessant chatter of my mind.

When I was suffering, I had **no guidance**, no one to tell me what was happening to me, no one to advise me on how to manage and get freedom from the **voice in my head**.

Therefore, I feel duty-bound to share my **experience**s through this book so that millions of people all over the world who may have **similar** sufferings due to their minds as I had may get relief with the techniques and knowledge mentioned in this book.

My intentions in writing this book are:

1) To inform and teach people of the working of their mind so that they can use it for blissful existence.

2) To give relief to people suffering from mental problems

3) To reduce suicides and attempt to suicide rates all over the world

All the techniques and activities mentioned in this book have been tried and tested several hundreds of times. This book is written out of **experience and not theory**.

Listed below is a description of some of the symptoms of my suffering. I have written the same so that the reader may **connect or identify** with some of them and then use the knowledge contained in this book to overcome them.

Symptoms and my story in brief

Many times, my **hyper-active** mind would race very fast, and I would find it difficult to slow it down. I would shout and yell to my parents that my mind is working very fast, I wanted to slow it down, but it was not happening.

Sometimes, a single thought used to get **stuck** in my mind, and I would find it impossible to get rid of it. The more I would try not to think of it, the more it would persist.

On several occasions, my mind would take full control of me and make me do things even if I didn't want to do them. I used to feel like a **puppet** of my mind, helpless and out of control over my life.

Often, I would get fed up with the **voice in my head**. The voice would just not shut up. It would incessantly babble and chatter to my misery and dismay. The more I tried to shut it up, the **louder** it would get.

On most days, I would wake up in the morning with a **negative or paranoid stream** of thoughts which would attract more of the same, and I would feel **exhausted** within 10 minutes of waking up.

The whole day I would roll in the thoughts of some past **regret** or future **stress and fear**.

All the above **symptoms** were there because I had absolutely no '**present moment awareness**'. I was living my life completely identified with my mind. It was never quiet, calm, or serene. It was continuously **jumping** without any relief. I was completely **attached** to my mind - the attachment was even stronger than super glue.

My mind was in control of me as a king is in control of his servants. I was constantly running here and there to satisfy its **insatiable desires and nuisances**.

Then the inevitable happened. I had a **nervous breakdown**. I was hospitalized and **sedated**. While sedated, there was relief, but as soon as I would gain full waking consciousness, all my obsessive and compulsive thoughts would capture me again with even more force and vengeance.

I started thinking of suicide. I thought that it was the only way out of this torture. The mental trauma was even worse than physical pain. I would think hours about which method to use for suicide. I did some basic research for a painless suicide. Suicide seemed a better option compared to the suffering of the mind.

Freedom from the Monkey Mind

But God was kind. Timely **help** gave me direction and put me on the path of healing. I learnt **yoga, meditation, prayer, mantras,** and several other things, which helped me recover completely. I have described a lot of it in my books—'**High on life', 'Kefi', and 'Crying Baby Watching Hen'.** (I recommend the reader read these books to get more information and understanding on the topic of mental health)

Today, I am the master of my mind. My mind **serves** me rather than I serve it.

I endeavour to share this knowledge through the tried and tested 22 techniques that I learnt and practiced getting relief and **mastery over my mind.**

Do **try it** and see it for yourself!

Table of Contents

Introduction

Human beings are experiencing one of the biggest **epidemics** in the history of mankind. No, I'm not talking about corona. I'm talking about the epidemic of the **uncontrolled**, untamed, and untrained mind.

Thinking has become a dreaded **disease**. As I write this book, the greatest illness in the world, the number one killer, is not cancer or heart attack but stress and anxiety due to the **inability** to tame and control the mind.

Millions around the world are suffering from overthinking, negative thinking, and depressive thinking. For these people, theirs minds are a **curse**, as they are constantly playing **havoc** on their health and happiness.

Unfortunately, **nobody** seems to be taking this epidemic seriously. One of the reasons for not taking cognizance of it is that science cannot **measure** it or collect statistical data about it. Nobody has seen it, touched it, or measured it. We are dealing with something **formless, colourless, weightless**, tasteless. Anything we know has come from the direct experience of the enlightened yogis and saints who have encountered different dimensions of existence and have experienced this thing called the mind.

Please note, I am not suggesting that the mind is an evil thing. It is one of the most **amazing principles** on this planet. However, it has evolved slightly in the **wrong direction**, making it difficult for us humans to enjoy it and use it in a better and profitable way.

If left unchecked, the human race is not threatened by any external force. It is challenged by this most **mysterious entity** called the mind. This entity could be the difference between the survival of our race or its **destruction**.

This book is a step towards helping people understand their minds better so they can use them **productively**. It is all about the workings of the mind and how to use that knowledge in our **favour**. It is about getting freedom from the negative **aspects** of the mind.

This book is divided into **two** parts. The first part introduces the reader to 22 **characteristics** of the mind. The second describes 22 **activities** that will help the reader break the continuous chatter of the mind, giving relief and freedom from the incessant rant of the voice in the head.

Even though the ability to think was one of the biggest gifts of God given to mankind, in its **present avatar,** it has become a curse.

This curse needs breaking. It needs lifting.

This book is an answer to getting **freedom** from this curse.

Important notices

Before we begin reading the main contents of this book, here are some important notices to put it in perspective and give an idea as to what to expect from this book and what not to.

Note 1

Every activity/technique in this book will not work for every person. There is no one size fit all method. Depending upon a person's basic nature and nurture, some techniques will work more than others. Readers should try each activity and decide for themselves which one suits them better.

Note 2

The topic of the mind and its issues is a vast topic, and no one book can address all the aspects of it. I have written three other books that touch upon this topic. **'High on life'** specifically deals with depression, **'Crying baby watching hen'** deals with one meditation technique that can permanently solve many mental issues, and **'Kefi'** deals with happiness. The reader is encouraged to read these books to get an all-around view of their mental problems and the solutions.

Note 3

All techniques mentioned in this book are very effective for giving instant immediate relief from any obsessive, negative, compulsive, or depressing thought which may have overwhelmed a person to the extent that they are rendered helpless or in the grip of such a thought.

However, please note that these techniques give **temporary relief only** while the activity is being performed. For permanent relief, the reader should read my other books; having said that, the efficacy of instant

xxiv   *Freedom from the Monkey Mind*

relief should not be undermined even though it may be temporary in nature. These techniques have the power to save a person's life when that person gets caught in a suicidal or destructive thought which they cannot get rid of.

Note 4

Nomenclature:

I have used the words consciousness and awareness as synonyms.

At many places, I have used the nomenclature—brain-mind duo. Even though both are different, as explained in characteristic no. 17 of the mind, they are inextricably linked and related. For example, when the brain is overwhelmed with sensory data and hangs, the corresponding effect is that the mind also hangs. Therefore, there could be places where I have used these terms interchangeably since the result is the same. Please note that the mind is not accessible without the brain, and the brain is useless without a mind to guide it. There is a direct relationship between the mind and the brain.

Thus, when I say that the 'mind was overwhelmed', it can be read as 'the brain was overwhelmed' and vice versa.

Note 5

At many places, I have repeated words and concepts. I included repetition intentionally to emphasize those ideas and points so the reader can absorb some of the keywords more efficiently. Further, in some places, I have used several synonyms of a word to describe the same concept, belief, or idea. I also did this purposely because different people from different parts of the world relate to different words more easily.

Twenty-Two Important Characteristics of the mind

1) **One thought at a time.**

   The mind can think, process, and focus on only **one** thought at a time. It cannot do **parallel processing** or think of many things at the same time. However, in common experience, we sometimes feel that the mind is doing many things at one moment in time - this is **an illusion** caused due to **the fast speed** at which the mind works.

   Therefore, if we want our minds to get away from one thought or **obsession**, we can forcefully focus on **another** thought or object.

2) **The mind can exist only in two states.**

   The mind can be in only two states. Either it can be in an **active state** where it is continuously jumping from one thought to another, rolling in the past or future, labelling and judging every sensory input and thereby creating **chaos, stress, fear, and anxiety**. Or, it can be in an **inactive/passive state** where it is in a state of 'Present Moment Awareness' –**THE NOW**. In this state, it becomes **still, calm, and alert,** resulting in **peace, serenity, tranquillity, and clarity**.

Therefore, whenever we become aware that the mind is in the active state of continuous chatter, we can deliberately bring it to the passive state of the 'present moment awareness' where its chattering stops.

3) **The untrained and untamed mind.**

By default, an untrained and untamed mind is in the **active state** of rolling in past **regrets** and future **stress** and fear and creating all kinds of confusion, chaos, and difficulties. In this state, it is constantly **agitated** and cannot think clearly.

Therefore, if you want the mind not to be in its **default chaotic** untrained state, we can train it to be in the 'present moment awareness state' where it becomes **STILL and QUIET**.

4) **Conduct when danger is perceived.**

If the mind perceives danger to **life or limb**, it stops rolling in its regular habitual thinking pattern and completely **focuses** on the danger with full alertness. When faced with any danger, the mind focuses all **its energy** on **saving** and protecting the body from that danger. The mind gives **precedence** to life-saving activities compared to other regular **mundane activities**. For example—if a poisonous snake is in front of you, your mind will immediately sense danger to the body and let go of all other activities. It will become **intensely alert**, not losing sight of the snake and will become extremely aware of the present moment without any chatter and blabber.

Therefore, if we intentionally do any act that the mind interprets as putting our body in danger, the mind immediately stops all its other activities. It stops its **incessant** rolling and chattering and comes to the **rescue** of the body by being absolutely alert and in the present moment and ready for fight or flight.

5) **Overwhelmed with sensory information**

When the mind is **overwhelmed and flooded** with information in the form of sensory information, it temporarily **hangs** or gets **suspended**, just like a computer hangs if too many commands are given to it in a short time. During this hung state, the mind is **unable** to roll in the past or future and cannot continue its incessant chatter.

Therefore, if we purposely overwhelm our mind with any activity, we can cause it to be temporarily hung and thus get freedom from its constant chatter and rant for the time of that activity.

6) **Attention and energy**

Our mind gets its energy from our **attention** towards it. Accordingly, it **loses** its power and energy if we stop feeding it with our **indulgence**. Our attention and attachment towards it are the **fodder** and **nutrition** for the mind.

In the default untrained state, the mind **sucks** all the energy of a person towards itself. It **love**s attention.

Hence, a regular common person with an untrained mind **identifies** themself 100 percent with their thoughts.

Therefore, if we **starve** the mind of our attention, we starve it of its food, and we thereby weaken its influence and nuisance over us.

7)   **Master or Servant?**

In the default untrained state, the mind is the master, and the body is the servant. The mind completely takes over the body. It is in this state that we human beings feel out of control. We experience the nuances of the mind and are unable to break away from them. When we shine our awareness and watch our mind, it is forced to come to a 'state of presence' where it is cannot roll in its chaotic past memories and future imagined anxieties. In such a situation, we are able to control and manage it to our advantage and use its abilities for our benefit.

Therefore, if we want our mind to be our servant and under our control, we must voluntarily bring it to the 'present moment awareness' where it gets incapacitated to chatter and roll, and we can get relief from its continuous banter.

8)   **Evolution of the mind**

The mind has been evolving over hundreds of millennia. In its present date **avatar**, the mind has evolved to be **paranoid**, fearful, and angry.

Therefore, if we can make the mind **still and quiet** by shining our awareness on it, then the mind cannot create fear, anxiety, and stress.

9) **The mind loves to Judge**

The mind loves to judge, compare, and label all its sensory inputs in the form of objects, emotions, situations, etc.

Therefore, if we can prevent the mind from doing what it loves to do by ignoring it or starving it of our attention, it is unable to judge and compare and create chaos in our mind.

10) **Limitations of the mind**

The mind has a **limitation** - it can only think in terms of **objects and forms**. The mind cannot think of anything which is **formless** and cannot think of 'No-thing' (not a thing).

Therefore, if we push the mind to think of anything formless, the mind is unable to do so and, in its endeavour to make an object out of something objectless, it loses power and focus over whatever else it was doing at that time. This way, we can **divert,** distract, or channelize the mind from any compulsive, obsessive, habitual addicted thinking to anything we want.

So if we feed our mind with sensory input without any object, it is unable to **make sense** of it, and it puts all its energy into trying to decipher the objectless input.

11) Disidentification from our mind

Most of us completely **identify** with our minds. However, if we disidentify ourselves from the mind, it loses control over us. We can disidentify by **watching** and **observing** our mind as something that is **different** from our true essence and our true self. That true self is our awareness and consciousness or the **divine in us.**

Therefore, if we watch our mind(thoughts) as an entity different from ourselves, the mind cannot play havoc with us.

12) Mind thinks in duality

The mind thinks in **binary** or **extremes or polarity**. It labels all sensory inputs in two categories - a positive category of good/pleasurable/cravings or a negative category of bad/pain/aversion. It cannot think in terms of grey or shades of grey.

This duality creates a lot of problems. By understanding this trait of an untrained mind, we can intentionally train the mind to be in the **middle**. We can train the mind to be in **equanimity**. We can teach it to be neither on the **positive side** or the **negative.**

This training prevents the mind from creating any feelings or emotions or craving or resistance for any sensation experienced by it.

Therefore, if we train the mind not to judge and label and sensory input, it loses its power to move in opinions, views, biases, and perceptions, and we get relief from its continuous judgement and labelling.

13) **Gibberish Input and confusion**

The mind can work only if it finds something **understandable** (which makes sense to it). If we feed the mind with something it cannot understand, it cannot work properly. It gets **confused and ineffective**. If we feed it with anything that it cannot grasp, then it gets busy trying to decode and make sense of what it is receiving, and it '**lets go**' of all other activities to make sense of the new **unintelligible** information.

Therefore, if we purposely feed the mind with unintelligible (Gibberish) data or sensory input, the mind gets busy to make sense of it, and in that endeavour, it moves away from all other activities which it was earlier doing. This can be used to distract the mind from any negative, obsessive, habitual, compulsive, destructive, damaging or harmful activity which it was previously doing.

14) **What the mind resists, it persists.**

A thought persists if we resist. It will persist with us either if we feed it by **welcoming** it and desiring more of it, OR if we **suppress or repress** it and desire it to go away. One of the effective ways to get rid of any thought is neither to welcome it nor to push it away. Just observe it **without any desire**.

Therefore, we should neither resist nor welcome any thought or feeling or sensation. If we accept all or any thoughts without suppressing, repressing, or craving, then that thought slowly loses power and disappears.

15) **The mind is a storyteller**

The mind loves storytelling. It is a **dramatist** - it likes importance and loves to exaggerate. It likes to make a mountain out of **a molehill** and craves to get full 100 percent attention from a person. It fancies being in the **spotlight**. The mind can **never** be satisfied - it is always demanding and **crying** for something. If you satisfy one of its demands, it throws up two more.

Therefore, we should learn to **ignore its stories** and not to feed it with our interest. If ignored, the mind loses power over us. The mind then cannot suck all our attention and energy towards itself, which gives us freedom from its continuous chatter.

16) **Mind under a spotlight**

When the mind is being watched or is in the **spotlight**, it becomes very alert and comes into the present moment awareness. During that time, it suspends or stops all the other activities. The mind is at **its best behaviour** when it is being **judged.**

Therefore, if we put ourselves in a situation where we are under a spotlight and in front of people who are judging us, like on **stage** or at a seminar, our mind leaves all other work and becomes alert under the spotlight to be in the total awareness state.

17) **Mind and Brain are not the same things**

Mind and brain are not the same things. The relationship between the brain and the mind is best understood by learning the relationship between the **hardware and software** of a computer. The brain is the hardware, and the mind is the software. To access the software, one must go through the hardware. Alone, both are **useless.** Together they **are matchless**.

The brain and mind are **inextricably** connected, meaning that when we **influence** one of them, the other also gets affected. If we change our thoughts, the brain reacts accordingly, and vice versa. If the brain hangs due to an **overflow** of sensory information, so does the mind. If the mind perceives danger, the brain acts accordingly.

Therefore, if we hang the brain on purpose by overwhelming it with sensory information, the mind also hangs due to this **inseparable** relationship between the two.

18) **Reduce sensory input, reduce the chatter of the mind**

Since the mind is in a continuous process of judging, comparing, and labelling all the sensory inputs it receives from the sense organs, if we **reduce or stop** the sensory inputs, the chatter also reduces or stops proportionately.

Therefore, if we do any act which causes any or all of our five senses to shut down, we can reduce the activity of the mind as it has less information to decipher.

19) **Association between the mind and the breath**

The mind and the breath are **closely associated**. What this means is that when we **change** our breathing rhythm, the mind follows and vice versa. Next time you experience any intense emotion, just watch and compare your **breathing pattern** with the pattern when you are not emotional.

You will notice that your breathing is different when you are angry, happy, in pain, feeling aroused, etc. When your breathing is long and deep, your mind is calm and serene, and when it is short and shallow, you are excited.

Therefore, we can use the breath **to manipulate and influence** our minds.

20) **Our mind is our ego.**

If you put your mind in a situation where it is **challenged to perform**, it will put all its energy and effort into that activity. If the mind is **dared to win** something or prove something, it takes that task very seriously, and it will try its best to complete, achieve, or accomplish that task as it doesn't like to **lose or fail**.

Therefore, if we challenge the mind for **glory**, we can be sure that the mind will let go of all other activities and focus only on that activity which will give it respect and admiration.

21) **Disobey our mind**

When we disobey our minds **intense desire** to do something, the will to disobey comes from an energy that is at a **higher pedestal** than our mind. This willpower to disobey comes from our pure consciousness awareness. Hence, if we want to get a **glimpse** of that power, wisdom, and intellect of our pure consciousness, we can do so by **STOPPING ourselves** from indulging in an intense desire.

Therefore, we can experience our pure awareness by using our willpower to disobey an intense desire of the mind.

22) **Thoughts don't belong to you.**

Have you ever thought—where do our thoughts come from?

It may surprise you to know that thoughts are **present everywhere** around you, just **like air**. Thoughts are **not created** by you, even though you may feel like that. You feel that way because you completely **identify yourself** with your thoughts. Thoughts are **guests.** What this means is that they do not have a permanent residence in you. Thoughts are like a **gypsy**, continuously moving in and out of your mind.

Thoughts are a part of the **collective consciousness** of the universe, and they pervade the entire universe.

Therefore, you must be able to **differentiate** between your thoughts (guests) and your true nature (our permanent residence).

Twenty-Two Activities to get Instant temporary relief from the Chattering Mind

Short description of the activity

In this activity, we use *hunger as a tool* to fool the mind into survival mode.

Characteristic of the mind used

In this activity, we use that trait of the mind which says that when the mind is in **survival mode,** it leaves all other work, including its habitual negative and obsessive thinking, and gets busy trying to avert the danger. The mind gives **top priority** to its survival compared to any other activity.

Detail Description

When the body is in a state of **emergency or danger**, the mind stops all its other work and focuses all its energy on the survival of the body and, therefore, itself. Thus, it stops its **default obsessive thinking**, overthinking, negative thinking and puts all its energy into trying to do something to avert the danger and save the body.

Hence, whenever we want to break a stream of obsessive thoughts, we can forcefully bring the mind into survival mode by starving our bodies.

This activity is very simple. Just skip a couple of meals and bring your body into a state of hunger.

I'm sure all the readers may have experienced this. When we are very hungry, we can't think straight. In some cases, we can't think of anything else but food.

Why is it like this?

When we skip a meal or two, the body sends an emergency **signal to the brain** saying that it needs nutrition. In reality, we will not die if we don't eat for a few days, but the brain is overwhelmed with distress signals from all over the body saying it needs nourishment. The **brain is fooled** into thinking that the body will perish if it is not given food. Thus, the mind, which is inextricably related to the working of the brain, gets into survival mode and focuses all its attention and energy towards satisfying the sensation of hunger, thus *letting go* of its default nature of obsessive negative thinking.

So by voluntarily being hungry, we can get temporary relief from the clutches of any obsessive, negative, or undesired activity that the mind was doing.

Try to think straight when you are very hungry—**you can't!**

Summary: We starve ourselves to force the mind into survival mode where the mind leaves all other work (obsessive, negative, destructive) and gets busy in activities that will be beneficial to save the body.

What is Sufi whirling?

Sufi whirling is a form of physically active meditation that originated among certain Sufi groups and is still practiced by the Sufi Dervishes of the Mevlevi order and other orders such as the Rifa'i-Marufi. ~ Wikipedia

(To understand Sufi whirling, please find a third party Youtube link at the end of this technique.)

Short description of the activity

In this activity, we open out our hands and swirl round and round till we feel extremely dizzy so as to confuse and overwhelm the brain and put the mind in a survival mode forcing it to divert all its energy to becoming alert and aware and in the present moment awareness to save the body from any harm.

Characteristic of the mind used

In this activity, we use the same principles as the ones used in 'Running activity'.

Principle 1—When we do any activity that the mind perceives could harm the body, then the mind becomes very alert and goes into survival mode to save the body from danger.

Principle 2—When we do any activity where there is a flow of a lot of sensory data, the mind hangs and lets go of all other sundry activities.

Detail Description

Sufi whirling was used as a meditative practice. Why?

Because thousands of people were able to connect with their true self and their divine consciousness through this physical activity.

Today we shall learn how these people were able to connect to their true nature through this practice.

The only thing that stands between us discovering our true divine nature and ultimate reality is our every chattering, every moving, ever disturbing monkey mind. Due to the incessant and continuous babble of the mind, we fail to realize and experience our divine consciousness, which lies behind this monkey mind.

When we twirl round and round for minutes and many times for hours, initially, the mind goes into survival mode as it is flooded with information that says that the body is feeling dizzy and unstable, and there is a possibility that it may fall down, injuring itself. In this initial stage, the mind leaves all its sundry work and becomes extremely alert in order to save the body from any harm.

As we continue to move round and round, after some time, with an overdose of sensory and confusing information, the mind hangs. It simply hangs. When it hangs, the chatter stops completely. In this complete silence of the mind, our true nature is revealed.

This revelation has led to thousands of people tasting the divine. This practice has led thousands of people to the state of Moksha or Nirvana (enlightenment).

When we use the phrase "our mind hangs", what we mean to say is that it stops jumping and bouncing around (active) and becomes completely STILL or frozen (inactive/hangs). This inactive mind is not a 'negative inactive' as it does not mean that the mind dies or stops being alive. It is a positive inactiveness, where the mind is present, but it is very STILL and QUIET, without any chatter. The word 'hang' is used in the same way as we use it when we say "our computer is hung", where the screen freezes but is still present.

Summary:

We perform Sufi whirling in order to confuse and overwhelm our minds into hanging. When the mind hangs, its chatter stops completely, and we can experience our true nature as well as get freedom from our minds clutches.

(Please find below a link of a third-party youtube video explaining Sufi whirling)

https://vishal-gupta.com/sufiwhirling

3 Sneeze

Short description of the activity

In this activity, we deliberately induce a sneeze to force the body to use all its power and energy to eject the foreign and irritant matter from our nostrils.

Characteristic of the mind used

When the body undergoes any stressful activity where the entire body becomes overloaded with sensory information, then all the energy of the body and the mind go into managing that activity and nothing else.

Detail Description:

The act of sneezing is a very stressful activity for the body. It's a very complex act where many things happen in the body to prepare the body for ejecting a foreign matter that has caused irritated the nostrils out of the body with force.

A sneeze travels at more than 100 km per hour. To generate that speed and that force, the body has to coordinate its muscles and other systems in the body in such a manner so it can create an environment that can eject an unrequired object from itself (nostril) at high speed. The irritant object in the nasal passage is perceived as a threat to the wellbeing of the body.

In a sneeze, the body goes into a temporary spasm, a tremor, shaking the mind out of its continuous stream of thinking.

At the beginning of a sneeze and during the sneeze, the body reallocates all the energy available to itself to generate that high level of power required to dispel the annoying foreign object out from the nostril.

Since so much energy gets used up in a sneeze, the mind has no energy to continue its habitual thinking, and a person feels relieved from the mind's chatter for the duration of that sneeze and a few seconds thereafter.

I am sure that many people may have experienced that after a sneeze (sometimes multiple sneezes), they feel tired; this is because to initiate and complete a successful sneeze, the body uses up a lot of its resources. In fact, the sneeze shakes the mind so vigorously that many people forget what they were conversing or discussing before the sneeze.

A sneeze is such a powerful act by the body that it renders the mind completely stunned, numbed, and incapacitated for a few seconds. Therefore, it is impossible to think while sneezing. You can either think or sneeze. You can't do both!

In addition, many people report that they feel a sense of relief and liveliness after a sneeze. This sense of relief is not because of the ejection of the irritant but due to the easing of the mind's chattering. It is similar to the relief we feel when our noisy window air conditioners are shut off for a few seconds.

Thus, a sneeze can be induced to break an obsessive thought which has been troubling us.

Try it. (But not during covid times 😊)

Summary:

We induce a sneeze which causes the entire body to get into a temporary spasm that shakes the body and mind, thereby snapping the mind out of its obsessive thinking.

4 Play a fast sport

Short description of the activity

In this activity, we play a fast sport like badminton, table tennis, or basketball to challenge the mind to be in a state of alertness and focus and to be able to play that sport successfully.

Characteristic of the mind used

In this activity, we use the attribute of the mind that if we do any movement requiring quick reflexes, the mind needs to be constantly alert, due to which it will not get any time to roll in its usual obsessive behaviour. Also, when the mind is challenged to perform to win or be successful, it puts all its effort into that activity as it does not like to lose or fail.

Detail Description

When we play a fast sport, we need to be extremely alert. We need to be focused like a hawk and fast like a cheetah.

If we let our guard down even for one second, it could cost us the game. The mind knows this and understands this. Also, the mind, which is our ego, likes to win.

This thinking forces the mind to be alert and in the present moment state. Once the mind is completely involved in the game, it takes it away from all its habitual brooding, thinking, fear, stress, and anxiety.

This is the real reason why millions of people around the world enjoy playing sports , as it gives them relief from the monkey mind.

Summary:

We play a fast sport to force the mind to be alert in order to be successful in playing that sport.

Talk Gibberish

What is gibberish?

Gibberish is unintelligible or meaningless speech or writing. It is speaking nonsense.

Short description of the activity

In this activity, we purposely talk gibberish (we make sounds or say things with no meaning to us) so that the brain gets confused and puts all its energy into deciphering the sounds and words, thereby letting go of any negative or unwanted work it was previously doing.

Characteristic of the mind used

The mind doesn't like confusion or unintelligent information. When the mind faces confusing data, it becomes fearful and insecure. This quality of the mind causes it to leave all other work it was busy doing and focus all its attention on decoding the gibberish data it is receiving.

Detail description

The mind gets uncomfortable with information that it cannot decipher or understand. When the mind faces unintelligent data, it becomes fearful and doubtful. The mind feels uneasy, awkward, and threatened when faced with a situation it cannot interpret, handle, or manage. This insecurity causes it to put all its energy into making sense of the unintelligent data; this is also one of the survival responses of the mind. When the mind finds itself in an unknown place or situation and doesn't know how to act or respond, it leaves all other work and becomes extremely alert to take itself out of that unfamiliar situation.

This attribute of the mind causes it to leave all other work that it was busy doing earlier and concentrate on decoding the gibberish data it is receiving.

Summary:

We talk gibberish to confuse the mind with unintelligent data, which forces the mind to leave all other work and become alert in the present moment awareness to decipher the data.

6 ⟩ *Watch your breath*

Short description of the activity

In this activity, we **watch and witness** our breathing at the **tip of our nostrils** from where the air goes in and out. By bringing our awareness and attention to our breathing, we **divert the energy** of our minds from its habitual overthinking to the present moment awareness of the watching of our breath.

Characteristic of the mind used

In this activity, we use the quality of the mind that the mind can only do **one thing at a time.** By forcing the mind's attention and energy on our breath, **we anchor** the mind on one activity and, thereby, take away its energy to do anything else. In this case, we take away its energy to roll in negative and obsessive thoughts of the past and future. The mind **cannot focus on two thoughts** at the same time. It can either focus on watching the breath, or it can focus on its default habitual thinking.

Detail Description

If there is one activity that is continuously happening in our bodies and for which we don't need any preparation, and which is free- it is our **breathing**.

Therefore, whenever we feel the need to divert our minds from negative or unwanted thinking, we can immediately take our awareness and alertness to the tip of our nose and feel the air going in and out. We must *just observe* and watch the air going in and out and **not judge or compare or label anything while doing so**. We have to watch the breathing completely unattached as if somebody else is breathing. We have to observe the movement of our breath as a person *looks at the movement of traffic* from the footpath. We do have to change our breathing pattern, nor do we have to manipulate it. We simply have to watch and witness it.

When we do this, the minds entire energy gets focused on watching the breath, and it loses its grip over the earlier obsessive thinking that it was doing.

Summary:

We watch and witness our breathing to force all the attention of the mind to this activity, thereby taking away the focus of the mind from a previous activity as the mind can work on only one activity at a time.

7 Menstruation / period *(women)*

Short description of the activity

In this activity, we use the menstruation phase of a woman as an occasion and opportunity to divert the attention of the mind from its habitual negative chatter to the ***present moment awareness*** by focusing it on the area of discomfort.

Characteristic of the mind used

When the entire energy of the mind is focused on **one thing**, the mind does not have any energy left to be focused on anything else. However, to use this characteristic, the mind needs an **object or sensation** or anything that it can perceive and **anchor itself**. The discomfort during menstruation becomes a sensation for the mind to anchor itself.

Detail Description

Most women undergo 4-5 days of discomfort and pain during their monthly periods. This phase can be used to **train the mind to focus** at a particular place or sensation, thereby giving relief to that person from the default incessant babble of the mind.

A woman should close her eyes and place her mind's attention and focus on the **area of discomfort**. By doing so, the entire energy of the mind is shifted from all other sundry work to this area. Once this stage is achieved, the women will find that the mind has stopped its uncontrollable and continuous babble, and there is a **great relief from the restless monkey mind**. By focusing the entire energy of the mind on the area of discomfort, the mind has no energy for doing any other work.

In addition to this, if the mind is trained not to label the discomfort as 'pain' or something undesirable and made to just observe the vibrations of that area without judgement, the so-called 'discomfort' will miraculous disappear, and the mind will also get trained to remain in equanimity.

As proficiency increases, a woman can have **more control** over the workings of the mind and will find it easier to direct the mind's energy for more productive and beneficial areas of life.

Summary:

We use the discomfort of the monthly period to focus the mind on the sensation, thereby forcing the mind to let go of any previous unwanted chatter.

8 Indulge in Adventurous activity

Short description of the activity

In this activity, we indulge in any adventurous activity or a risky activity to fool the mind into survival mode.

Characteristic of the mind used

When the mind perceives a threat to life from the information it gets from the sense organs, it gives the highest priority to its survival and, therefore, leaves all other work and becomes extremely alert and in the 'NOW moment' to avert that peril.

Detail Description

Many people love adventurous activities like rock climbing, parasailing, jumping from a plane, deep-sea diving, etc. These activities cause an adrenaline rush as they are risky and dangerous.

Many of these people will tell you that they love these activities even though a common person fails to understand why these people would put their lives in danger to indulge in these activities.

Today, I will share the secret of why people love these so-called adventurous pursuits.

These people love adventurous activities and sports because while performing them, they can experience the divine (even if it is for a few seconds). These people are able to taste their true nature while performing these activities even without knowing that they are doing so.

Let's take one example to understand this—bungee jumping.

When a person bungee jumps, for a few seconds, the brain-mind duo get into absolute survival mode. This happens because when the eyes give information to the brain that the body is falling a few hundred feet, the brain-mind interpret it as a danger to life, and they become absolutely alert and still in order to figure out how to save the body. It is in these few seconds that the mind's chatter shuts down completely, and a person can get glimpses of their true nature—which is pure joy and bliss. Please note that the only thing that prevents a normal person from experiencing their true nature is the 'jumping mind'. As and when this mind stops jumping, the veil that hides a person's true nature is lifted, and a person is able to experience the eternal and infinite Godliness within them.

Of course, certain hormones are also released, but the feeling of joy and bliss comes from the complete shutting down of the mind from its active babble, and it becomes extremely *quiet* and *alert* in the *"present moment awareness"*.

Summary:

We use adventurous sport as a *trigger* to bring the mind into survival mode, forcing the mind to become extremely *ALERT* and *STILL* and giving a person a glimpse of their true eternal nature.

9 Japa-mala

What is a japa mala?

A japa mala, or simply mala (Sanskrit: mālā, meaning 'garland'), is a string of prayer beads commonly used in Indian religions such as Hinduism, Jainism, Sikhism, and Buddhism for the spiritual practice (sadhana) known in Sanskrit as japa. Please see the adjacent image to get an idea of what a japa mala is.

Short description of the activity

In this activity, we use a beaded japa mala to focus our minds on the repetition of a mantra or an affirmation continuously till all the beads have been counted. A japa mala usually has 108 beads. (Why the number 108 is important is a topic for another time and another book.)

Characteristic of the mind used

The mind can only do one activity at a time. It can process only one thought at a time. Therefore, if we want the mind to stop thinking of something we don't like, we use our willpower to divert it to focus its energy on repeating a mantra or an affirmation. By using a japa mala, we are able to give the mind a goal to repeat a mantra for a certain number of times, thereby making the mind lose its grip over all other sundry activities.

Detail Description

The mind needs continuous work. It cannot sit idle. It is like a monkey that is jumping continuously. If we don't give it any positive work, it gets busy with its innate nature of destructive work. Therefore, to prevent it from doing its negative activities, we anchor it in a mantra and give it a goal to finish reciting a mantra 108 times.

As mentioned earlier, the mind cannot focus on two things at the same time. Therefore, If we keep the mind busy with one work, it will not be able to do any other. If we keep the mind busy doing some productive work, it will not have the time, energy, and space to do any harmful work.

Therefore, knowing this, we focus our mind on reciting a spiritual mantra. If there are people who do not know any mantra, they can recite any affirmation they believe in. The whole point of doing this is to keep the mind busy doing some work.

Summary:

We use a japa mala to anchor our minds on any mantra or affirmation so that the mind gets busy doing the same and lets go of any other activity.

⟨10⟩ *Kali face*

Who is Kali?

Kali is a Hindu **goddess. Kali is the chief of the Mahavidyas, a group of ten Tantric goddesses who each form a different aspect of the Mother goddess Parvati.**

Kali has been worshipped by devotional movements and tantric sects as the Divine Mother, Mother of the Universe, Adi Shakti or Parvati. Shakta Hindu and Tantric sects additionally worship her as the ultimate reality or Brahman. Some also seen her as the divine protector and the one who bestows moksha or

40

liberation. Kali is often portrayed standing or dancing on her consort, the Hindu god Shiva, who lies calm and prostrate beneath her.

Short description of the activity

In this activity, we make a Kali face as shown in the image on the adjacent page and as described below. The making of this face causes the chatter in the brain to decrease or stop due to the position and state of the mouth and tongue.

Characteristic of the mind used

Certain parts of our bodies are connected to the brain in such a manner that they have a direct and profound effect on the activity of the brain and the movement of thoughts in the mind. One such body part is the tongue. The tongue is connected to the brains language centre and if often moves when we think. The movement is so slight that we cannot perceive it. However, the point is that when the mind is thinking, the tongue also moves as per the thoughts. If we intentionally stop the movement of the tongue by making it stiff, the movement of thoughts in the mind also reduces or stops. Additionally, if we bite the tongue, the intense pain caused therein breaks any or all stream of thoughts in the brain-mind duo.

Detail Description

I'm sure most of you readers may have experienced themselves or seen in others that when people are under the influence of alcohol or drugs or suffer from any brain-related issues like Alzheimer's or Parkinson's, their speech becomes slurred. What this means is that when the brain is not working normally, one of the first things to get affected is the tongue; this shows and proves that there is a significant connection between brain activity and the tongue.

We use this connection between brain activity and tongue movement to intentionally influence the tongue by making it stiff (stopping its movement), which influences the mind (reducing or stopping the movement of thoughts).

To make a Kali face, we open our mouths wide and stick out our tongues like the Goddess Kali to stop the thinking activity in the brain-mind duo. Please see the adjacent image of Goddess Kali to appreciate why this activity is called Kali-face.

A wide open mouth and a stiff tongue are linked to brain activity in such a manner that they decrease or stop the movement of thoughts in the mind.

Another thing that can snap a person out of obsessive thinking is biting the tongue. If we bite it, the pain and the act itself sends a very strong pain signal to the brain, which shakes it up completely and the brain-mind duo loses grip over all the work they were doing earlier. I am sure the readers may have experienced the agony of a tongue bite.

Summary:

We make a Kali face and intentionally stop the movement of the tongue, which directly stops the movement of thoughts in the mind as the tongue and brain activity are closely connected.

11 Running

Short description of the activity

In this activity, we run or sprint short distances at high speed to overwhelm the brain with sensory information and force it into survival mode.

Characteristic of the mind used

When we run, we use two principles of the mind.

Principle 1—When we do any activity that the mind perceives could harm the body, then the mind becomes very alert and goes into survival mode to save the body from danger.

Principle 2—When we do any activity where there is a flow of a lot of sensory data, the mind hangs and lets go of all other sundry activities.

Detail Description

Many dancers or long-distance runners will tell you that while dancing or running, a stage comes when they feel that they are no more doing that activity. They feel like the act of dancing and running is happening on its own without their interference. These people will tell you that, at this stage, they feel divine, blissful, and have a joy that they cannot express in words.

Why do they feel like this?

They feel this way because the mind hangs and there is zero chatter. When the chatter stops, these people can experience their higher self, their true nature, and their ultimate reality. This reality cannot be explained in simple words, and therefore I am not going to go into detail about it. It is sufficient to say that they experience the divinity in them.

When we run, at first, the mind becomes very alert because it has to save the body from falling, tripping, getting into accidents, etc. Most of us consider running is an easy act. Well, for the brain, it is a very challenging, difficult, and energy-consuming act as it has to work every second with full awareness to keep the body upright and safe from any obstacle or accident or mishaps.

Second, as we continue to run, a stage comes when the brain-mind duo get overwhelmed with sensory information, especially from the eyes and ears. This flood of information is due to the continuous effort required by the brain and mind to keep the body out of danger and accidents by processing all the information at top speed. However, there is a limit to the processing speed of the brain and mind, and if this speed is exceeded, they hang. Please note that keeping the body upright is a significant task for the brain as it needs to get information from every part of the body, especially from the fluid in the ears, which maintain balance, and from the legs and eyes, etc.

For many people running is an addiction. Why?

For millions around the world running is a joyful and stress relieving activity. Why?

Because when people run, their mental chatter and thoughts of anxiety and stress vanish. Their thoughts relating to their various problems that they kept overthinking about temporarily disappear or shut down. Consequently, these people experience an amazing feeling of calmness, bliss, and harmony.

Please note. Due to running, the problems don't disappear. What disappears for that period of time is the constant thinking of that problem. Interestingly, most runners don't understand why they love the activity of running.

I hope this chapter proves as an eye-opener to them.

Try it!

Summary:

We run to force the mind into alertness and survival mode and then overwhelm it with sensory information to cause it to hang, thereby getting freedom from its incessant babble.

Short description of the activity

In this activity, we intentionally disobey our urge to do something.

Characteristic of the mind used

In this activity, we use the trait of the mind that every time we disobey our mind's desire to do something, our awareness increases. The strength and willpower to disobey our mind's desire comes from our pure awareness.

Detail Description

Normally, we live our lives 100 percent through our

minds. We feel we are our minds, and therefore whatever it desires or wants to do, we think of it as our own personal desire; hence we keep on doing it.

However, as discussed many times earlier, we are not our minds. We are our consciousness-awareness-soul which is not an object but energy that pervades the entire universe. This awareness is watching us all the time, and it is our true nature, our true self. However, when we identify with our minds, we are living through the whims and fancies of the mind and not through the intelligence of our awareness.

Thus, to get freedom from our minds, we can use the intelligence of this awareness by intentionally disobeying the urges or desires of the mind. Every time we disobey our minds, our awareness strengthens; it increases as we can only disobey when our awareness overpowers our minds.

The mind is constantly creating desires and urges. It would not be wrong to call our minds 'desire factories'. During an ordinary day, we get hundreds of urges. While some urges are important for our survival, such as the urge to have water or food, some urges are for relief or pleasure, such as the urge to scratch or to eat something sweet.

These urges can be used to our advantage for increasing our awareness and getting an upper hand on the working of the monkey mind.

When we feel an urge—for example—an urge to scratch somewhere on the body or sneeze, etc., instead of carrying out that urge, try to disobey that urge as much as possible. In those moments of disobeying, your awareness increases to a very high level, and you can disidentify from your mind.

Unfortunately, many things cannot be explained well enough in words and phrases and have to be tried out and experimented with for the reader to understand the true and correct meaning of the activity.

So, try this idea to appreciate the valuable meaning of the words of this activity.

The moment you get your next urge---maybe an urge to have coca-cola, or the urge to smoke, or have alcohol or any sweet, etc. -STOP.

STOP yourself from giving in to that urge. Just feel the urge and be in the present moment. Observe the urge with full awareness but don't express or indulge in that urge.

When you do this, you will experience a wonderful kind of freedom. You will feel free from the dominance and push from your controlling mind.

Summary:

Disobey any intense urge to increase the level of your pure awareness and to decrease the control of your mind over you.

(13) *Chaotic breathing*

Short description of the activity

In this activity, we deliberately **breathe chaotically** to break the stream of negative/obsessive thoughts. Chaotic breathing means breathing without rhythm. It means breathing **fast, slow, deep, shallow, and jerky** in successive breaths without any pattern.

Characteristic of the mind used

Our minds and our breathing are **closely related**. When one changes, so does the other. Therefore, using this knowledge, we change our breathing to change the state of our minds.

Detail Description

Sometimes we are possessed by a **flow of unwanted thoughts** that take control over us, and we are unable to free ourselves from that cycle of thought. To us, it seems as if that train of thought has completely captured our entire minds, and we cannot come out of it.

In such a situation, the more we try to escape or suppress or repress the thought, the more it boomerangs back with more power and vengeance.

To come out of this torturous situation, we need to **change the pattern** of our breathing. In fact, we should breathe without any pattern or rhythm. We should breathe in an uncertain chaotic manner.

Close your eyes and breathe chaotically for 2-3 minutes. Make sure that no two successive breaths are in rhythm. Breath in jerks.

When you open your eyes after a few minutes, you will experience that the stream of thought that was **bothering you is no more.** Use this window of freedom from the compulsive thoughts to practice other techniques like meditation or mindfulness to prevent the re-occurrence of that stream of thought.

Our minds **don't like confusion.** They like structure, rhythm, and certainty.

With chaotic breathing, the mind is thrown off balance. It is flooded with information that is confusing and puzzling. Thus, it diverts its energy into making sense of what is happening to the breathing and the body, and in doing so, it **lets go** of the stream of thought that it was attached to.

When our breathing is in a rhythm and continuous, our stream of thought is also in an unbroken flow of continuous rhythm. However, the moment we disrupt this rhythm, our thought flow also gets disrupted, and we can break away from the clutches and grip of that negative and unwanted thought stream.

Summary:

Knowing that our breath and the working of our minds are intrinsically related, we breathe chaotically without rhythm to shake the mind from its vicious, destructive thinking.

14 Yawn

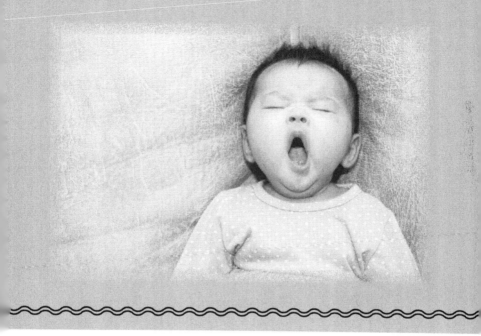

Short description of the activity

In this activity, we purposely induce a yawn which temporarily reduces the sensory information to the brain-mind duo.

Characteristic of the mind used

Certain physical acts reduce the sensory data to the brain-mind duo, causing them to become passive for the period of that act. Our body's physiology is such that when our mouths are wide open, most of our five senses either get temporarily suspended or work with a minimum efficiency.

53

Detail description

As you read this paragraph, induce a yawn. You will notice that your eyes will be forced to close. There will be no air movement in and out from the nose (there is a movement of air from the mouth). You will not be able to eat (taste) anything, and even though your ears cannot be physically closed like your eyelids, your hearing ability will diminish. (Try to hear someone while yawning, you will not be able to—try it.)

The eyes are the dominant source of sensory information in humans. On the other hand, noses provide dogs with their primary source of information. When this dominant source of sensory information gets closed, it reduces the brain activity and thus the mind activity.

A yawn creates a physiological situation where sensory data to the brain-mind pair stops or reduces to such an extent that the mind has no information to decipher or interpret. It gives the much-needed relief to a person from a negative thinking loop so that the person can use those precious 2-3 seconds after the yawn to break away from the vicious thinking stream of thought and direct the same somewhere else.

Further, when our eyes close, or we move into an area of darkness, our minds feel insecure and afraid as they don't get any sensory information from the outside world, so they don't know whether they will be safe. The mind feels a threat to its wellbeing and existence as it has no information that assures its safety. In such a situation, the mind goes into survival mode and stops jumping around and becomes still and alert in the present moment awareness, in anticipation of the slightest visual data to get its guarantee of safety and security.

This phenomenon is many times used in sexual games wherein one of the persons is blindfolded. As soon as that person becomes blindfolded, the mind immediately comes into the present moment awareness and enjoys all the bodily sensations that follow with extreme awareness.

Summary:

We intentionally induce a yawn to reduce the sensory input from all the senses, thereby feeding the mind with minimal data and causing it to reduce its judging, comparing, and labelling attitude.

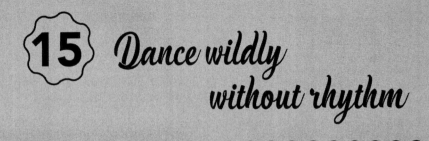

15 Dance wildly without rhythm

Short description of the activity

In this activity, we overwhelm and confuse the brain-mind duo with our erratic body/dance movements causing the duo to hang.

Characteristic of the mind used

We use two characteristics of the mind in this activity. The first characteristic is that when we confuse the mind with something, the mind gets busy with all its energy trying to understand and make sense of all the confusing stimulation it is receiving and therefore leaves all other habitual thinking work. Second, we use the trait that when the mind perceives danger to life or limb, it goes into survival mode and leaves all other work to attend to the perceived danger.

Detail Description

Close your eyes and dance erratically without any rhythm. Just shake your body wildly. The reason why I have asked you to dance erratically is to confuse the mind by feeding it with unexpected, unanticipated data. Whenever the mind gets confused, it reallocates all its energy to understanding and making sense of all the sensory information it is receiving.

The reason why I have asked you to close your eyes is because if your eyes are open, that sensory data will help the brain and mind to maintain balance and will give them a reference point to stabilize your body. With eyes open, the brain-mind duo is able to determine your body's bearings and location with respect to its surrounding. With the eyes closed, the mind is completely lost and goes into an overdrive mode to determine the body's posture, position, and safety. Consequently, the mind has to work twice as hard. The mind channelizes all its energy for the safety and survival of the body and lets go of all other work, including any long stream of depressive or negative thinking.

Please note that both the points, 1) To dance erratically and 2) To close your eyes, are equally important. If you miss one, you will not get the desired result.

Basically, the mind has to overwork to manage a body that is blind and moving without rhythm compared to managing a body that can see and is moving on a set rhythm or predefined steps.

Summary:

We dance erratically with eyes closed to confuse the mind so that it goes into an overdrive mode and determines the position and safety of the body, thereby letting go of all its habitual thinking for the time being.

16 Perform habitual daily activity differently

Short description of the activity

In this activity, we force the mind to be alert and in the present moment consciousness by giving it **a new sensory input** of which it is not habituated.

Characteristic of the mind used

Whenever we are learning something new, the mind is **forced into being alert**, focused, and in the present moment. However, as soon as something becomes a habit, the mind is no longer required to be alert and present, which leads the mind to go back to its restless and monkey nature. Therefore, by doing something differently, **we create a situation** that is new for the mind and thereby force it into the present moment and away from whatever was bothering us. We take back control of the mind from its clutches. We get freedom from its grip.

Detail Description

While doing any activity, when the mind is **challenged,** it is forced to be in the present moment to face that challenge. In contrast, when any activity becomes a habit, the minds continuous monitoring and alertness is not required.

Therefore, in this activity, we purposely, wilfully challenge the mind out of its habit by performing habitual acts in a different way.

For example: - if we brush our teeth with the right hand, as this has become a habit, we purposely brush our teeth with the left hand to challenge the mind to adapt to this new situation.

There are many habits we follow every day without even realizing that we are doing them because they do not require an alert mind. Let's list a few and see how we can do it differently-

Writing on paper- Write with the other hand

Holding any object- Hold with the other hand

Leisure walking in the park- Walk backwards for some time

Eating- Eat with the other hand

Playing any racket sport—Try to play with the other hand

Cleaning our bum with toilet paper—Try to clean with the other hand

Typing by seeing the keys- Type on the keyboard without looking at the keys

Every time you do the above activities, do them differently; this forces the mind into being alert and in the present moment awareness, and you can get temporary freedom from the chatter of the mind. Remember, once you can get temporary control over the chatter of the mind, you can then practice meditative techniques to slowly get complete control over the chattering mind. One of the powerful meditative techniques that you can use is detailed in my book "Crying Baby Watching Hen".

Summary:

We do habitual actions in a different way to provide the mind with a new situation, thereby forcing it into being alert and in present moment awareness.

17 Mindful hearing, eating and seeing

Short description of the activity

In this activity, we focus our mind's attention and energy on any one of our five senses to make the mind completely immersed, engrossed, and absorbed into the activity of that sense.

Characteristic of the mind used

We make use of the principle that the mind can think of only one thing at a time. Therefore, if our mind is stuck on something we don't want to think about, then we intentionally, using our willpower, focus the mind onto one of our senses and get the mind engrossed in the activity of that sense. This takes the mind away from what we don't want to think about and towards something we do want the mind to think about. Since the mind can think of only one thought at a time, it lets go of the earlier unwanted thought for the new desired thought.

How to do the activity?

Let us take the example of three of our senses, namely— sight, sound, and taste.

Sight—Focus the mind on seeing anything beautiful like a rose or a sunset or a tree or a bird and get completely involved in observing that sight. Watch that object as if there is nothing else in this world except that object. Study the minute details of that object, if possible, to understand and appreciate the beauty of that object.

Sound—Focus the mind on any pleasant sound or music. Let your mind get completely involved with that sound. Get so involved in the music that you forget everything else except that music.

Taste—While eating tasty food, bring your focus into your mouth and your taste buds. Feel the taste of the food or fruit on your tongue. Feel the rushing of the saliva and the burst of taste as you chew the food.

In all the examples above, we are focusing the mind purposely onto the activity of one of the senses so that the mind gets mindful in enjoying or observing that sense, and it loses its grip over any other unwanted negative activity which it was doing previously.

Summary:

We focus our minds on any one of our senses and make it completely engrossed in it, thereby making the mind 'let go' of the previous negative thought and replace it with a positive desired thought.

Short description of the activity

In this activity, we watch and witness our thoughts without getting involved with them. We watch it as another entity (which it is), and we remain aloof from it by just observing and witnessing it without desiring or suppressing any particular thought.

Characteristics of the mind used

We use the feature of the mind that if we starve our thoughts of our attention, then they lose power over us and fade away. If we don't interfere or get involved with our thoughts, they become weak as their food and power come from our involvement and attention. Once they become weak, they lose control over us, and we can experience freedom from their power and command.

Detail description

Our minds trouble us because we are completely identified with our minds. We think that we are our thoughts; we live 100 percent **in** our thoughts, **by** our thoughts, and **for** our thoughts. These thoughts get energy and power from our attention. If we don't give them our consideration, they lose power, and they lose their grip over us.

If we realize that our thoughts are different to our real self, then we can create a distance between our pure awareness (our true self) and the thoughts (not our true self) flowing through us. We can disidentify with our thoughts. We can understand that we are not our thoughts. In this activity, instead of inviting, rolling, or escaping from any thought, we just remain aloof and watch them as a bystander watches the traffic flow standing on the footpath.

Basically, we ignore our thoughts. When we starve our thoughts of our active participation with them, they fade out, giving us freedom from their chattering

Summary:

We ignore our thoughts by not getting involved with them and thereby starve them of our attention which weakens them, and we can experience freedom from their control.

Note: Watching, witnessing, and observing our thoughts is not the same as giving attention to our thoughts. Attention means becoming involved with our thoughts and either craving and enjoying a particular thought or suppressing and detesting any. In contrast, witnessing and watching means observing our thoughts without interfering or getting involved with them.

Short description of the activity

In this activity, we learn something new, as the mind has to be alert and focused to learn that new thing.

Characteristic of the mind used

Whenever we do any activity which requires the active and alert participation of the mind, the mind has no option but to leave all its default miscellaneous work and to put its energy into doing that activity.

Detail Description

Learning something new forces the mind to be in the vigilant and focused present moment awareness state.

When you learn something new, the mind has no option but to be very attentive, vigilant, and watchful. In contrast, when we do things out of habit, the mind is not required to be attentive. Let's take an example to understand this.

Example—Driving a Car

When we first learnt to drive, our minds had to be extremely alert so that we didn't run over someone and get into any kind of accident. However, once driving became second nature and a habit, we could drive hundreds of miles without even realizing so.

When we do something out of habit, the mind has very little to do, and everything works on auto-pilot mode. In contrast, when we do something new, the mind must be fully in alert and attentive mode to learn and understand that new thing.

So, learn a new skill or anything which you didn't know before. Learn to cook a new dish. Learn to play a new sport. Learn a new feature on your mobile phone - anything that forces the mind to be in an alert mode to understand that new information.

Summary:

Learn a new skill to force the mind in the attentive and alert mode, thereby making the mind leave its natural neurotic nature.

20 Stare into infinity with your eyes open

Short description of the activity

In this activity, we stare into the vast open objectless sky without any aim to look at any object or thing so that we starve the mind of any meaningful information that it can judge, label, or interpret.

Characteristic of the mind used

The mind can only think in terms of objects. Without any form or object, the mind does not know what to do.

Without any object, the mind cannot judge, compare, or label anything. If we starve the mind of any object to think about, it becomes weak, and it loses grip over us.

Detail Description

Normally, whenever we see something, our eyesight converges on that object.

Once the image of that object interacts with our mind as information, the mind immediately gets busy retrieving all the information we have about that object and gets into a cycle of judgement, comparison, and labelling of that object as either good or bad.

Suppose we see a red flower. The mind will immediately start to judge whether the red colour is good or not, the flower is beautiful or not, the flower is big or small, or it is as good as its neighbouring flower, etc.

Suppose we see the face of a person we know, immediately the mind will retrieve the information of the person from all the past experiences and label that face as a pleasant face and desirable face or a bad and undesirable face.

The converse is also true. If we starve the mind of any object, then it does not get any information to work upon and, therefore, it cannot judge, evaluate, and brand anything. This starvation of sensory information weakens its monkey nature, and it loses grip over us.

To perform this activity, sit on a bench and stare into the infinity of the sky with empty eyes. To understand what I mean by the phrase 'empty eyes', recollect the look of the eyes of a madman or an infant. Both have emptiness in their eyes.

Remember not to look at the clouds or birds or any other object that may be in the sky. Just stare into the vast blueness and emptiness of the sky. Your eyes should not fall upon any object. Your eyesight should be parallel without converging onto any object. Your eyes should just **SEE**, without any motive, aim, goal, or intention.

After a few minutes, the mind's chatter will reduce or stop because you would have starved the mind of any sensory information that it could process and judge.

Summary:

We stare into the vast objectless sky to starve the mind of any information that it can use or process. When the mind doesn't receive any information to process, its chattering reduces, and we feel a sense of relief and peace in our being.

21 *Sex / masturbate*

Short description of the activity

In this activity, we indulge in self-pleasure (masturbation) or sexual pleasure with our partners to overwhelm the body and mind with sensations leading it to hang due to sensory overload.

Characteristics of the mind used

In this activity, we use the principle that when the brain and body go into overdrive mode and get flooded with sensations and information requiring a lot of attention on a priority basis, then the mind stops all other activities and gets busy handling the body and brain. I am only distinguishing the brain from the body here to show that in sex, and more specifically during an orgasm, it is the brain that gets overwhelmed with information. The brain secretes several kinds of hormones and becomes the epicentre for the pleasure experienced by that person. The brain-mind duo hangs due to the flooding of excess sensory information to the brain. Remember that the pleasure of sex happens between the ears (brain) and not between the legs.

Detail description

Sex is a very intense act. So many things happen in the body that it would be impossible to list and describe all of them. I'm sure that even doctors and scientists with their hi-fi technology don't know about all the possible things that happen during an orgasm.

When we indulge in foreplay, our whole body experiences a heightened state of awareness and feeling. Every millimetre of the body erupts with the sensation of pleasure. There is a flood of hormones and other chemicals in our bloodstream. During an orgasm, the brain becomes bombarded with sensations from every inch of the body. There is a significant flow of information all over the body, which makes the brain hang, causing the mind to shut down from its relentless chatter.

In fact, one of the reasons we feel pleasure during an orgasm is because the mind becomes completely still and quiet, giving us a glimpse of our true nature and our divine selves. Some wise people have compared orgasms as the closest point to enlightenment, and that is why people feel a sense of joy and bliss.

The point I am making is that the feeling of bliss during an orgasm is more because of the stopping of the mind as opposed to the stimulation of the nerves or the release of the hormones. To support my argument, if hormones were released, but the mind chatter was going on, the mind would create doubt, suspicion, guilt, fear, and anxiety and would render the effect of the hormones ineffective.

Thus, any obsessive stream of thoughts can be effectively broken by sensory overload through a sexual act.

Summary:

We indulge in foreplay and sexual activity to overwhelm the brain and mind with sensory information causing the mind to hang and giving us freedom from the mind's chatter.

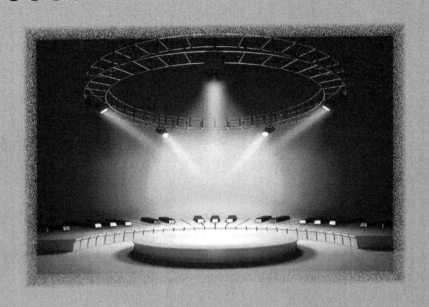

Short description of the activity

In this activity, we put our minds (our egos) in the spotlight in front of an audience. We purposely put ourselves in a situation where we are open to being judged and criticized.

Characteristic of the mind used

Our mind is our EGO. Our egos like to be in the limelight. It always likes to be right and a winner. When we are alone, our minds behave differently to when we are in a group or a crowd. When you are alone, your mind knows that there is no one to judge it and, therefore, it is not very alert to external judgement. However, when we are in a spotlight like on a stage or amongst friends at a party, or in a crowded market, our mind is very alert and in the 'present moment awareness' because it knows many people are watching and judging it and, therefore, it needs to be on its best behaviour.

Detail description

In this activity, we avoid being alone. We go to any place where there are people to judge us.

The mind has a different power over us when we are alone. In isolation, the mind uses all its energy to control us. We completely identify with our thoughts as the mind has no other distraction, diversion, or work; this changes when we are with people or in a crowded place where the mind has a lot of distractions and where it is open to being judged and commented upon.

So, whenever we are alone and want to break our negative thinking cycle, we should immediately leave that place and go to a friend's house or any crowded place where we are open to being judged on our conduct and behaviour. Basically, we should not leave ourselves alone.

Once we have company, our mind becomes very alert about its behaviour, performance, and action. Our mind (our ego) has a reputation to protect. It likes to be on its best behaviour when it is in front of people as it has its honour and prestige at stake.

Therefore, by creating a situation where the mind gets concerned about its behaviour, respect, honour and prestige, we force it to be alert and, thereby, release itself from any other futile or destructive work in which it was previously engaged.

Summary:

We avoid being alone and go to places where there are people who can judge us, thereby forcing the mind to be alert and in its best behaviour.

Review of the essence of all the 22 Activities

All the activities mentioned in this book do one or more of the ten things mentioned below

1) **Create or force the mind into 'present moment awareness'.**

   In the **'present moment awareness state'— 'the Now state'**, the mind cannot roll in the past or future. It cannot go into the mode of regretting the past and being in fear of the future. In the present moment, the mind becomes still. The chatter ceases.

2) **Starve the mind of attention**

   The mind can only work upon us when we give it attention. It can only grip us when we identify ourselves completely as the mind. If we ignore the mind and starve it of our attention and energy, it cannot influence us in any significant way. If we realize that we are not our mind and that our real self is different from our thoughts and mind, then the mind loses its power to trouble us.

3) **Overwhelm the mind with sensory information**

   When the mind is overwhelmed with sensory information, it hangs. When the mind hangs, it cannot chatter or do any of its habitual obsessive negative thinking work.

4)   Confuse the mind with unintelligent input

When we feed the mind with either unintelligent input (Gibberish) or with information that has no form, name, or quality, it gets confused. This confusion leads the mind to put all its energy into making sense of the unintelligent data and thereby let loose of its earlier rolling thoughts.

The mind can think only in terms of objects and forms. It can work in its normal innate state only when it can understand something.

5)   Wilfully focus the mind on a particular thought or object

The mind cannot do parallel processing. It can process only one thought at a time. Hence, if we make it busy with one particular thought, automatically, it loses grip over all other thoughts.

6)   Trick or influence the mind into survival mode

The mind gives its highest priority to life-saving activities. Consequently, whenever the mind perceives anything or any situation as dangerous, it becomes absolutely alert, attentive, and focused on the danger and goes into survival mode, thereby letting go of all other habitual obsessive and destructive thinking. When the mind is in survival mode, it makes saving itself from the threat the highest priority over any other activity.

7) **Use the inextricable connection between breath and mind or brain and mind**

Some of the activities indirectly influence the mind to stop its negative stream of thoughts by using the inseparable connection between the breath and the mind. These activities either focus on watching the breath or wilfully change the rhythm of the breath, which changes or breaks the thought stream. Similarly, you can use the connection between the brain and mind.

8) **Reduce sensory input via the five senses**

Reducing the sensory information from the five senses to the brain causes the mind to reduce its constant and continuous interpretation of the sensory information, resulting in reduced chatter.

9) **Challenge the mind (our EGO) to perform**

If we challenge or dare our mind to succeed or win in any activity, then it takes that activity very seriously and makes it a matter of prestige and honour. So, it puts its entire energy behind the challenging activity by being extremely alert, focused, and attentive. Remember-The mind hates losing or being a failure.

10) **Put the Mind under a Spotlight**

The mind is very concerned about its respect, honor, and reputation. Thus, if it is put in a situation where it knows that it's being closely watched and judged, then it becomes very alert to avoid doing anything that can result in embarrassment, shame, or humiliation.

Mind map of the review of the Activities

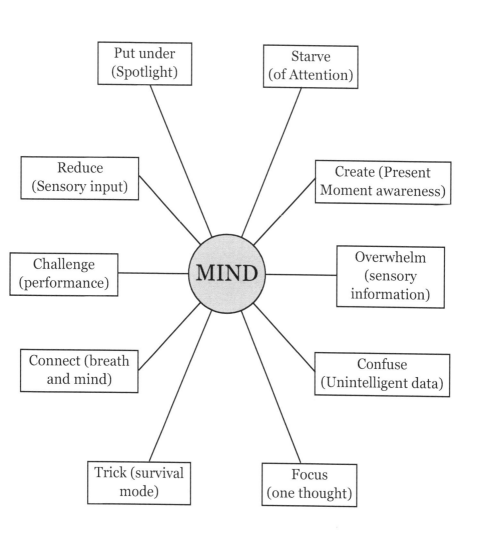

Worksheet

Now that you have finished reading this book, check whether you have understood and absorbed the information given herein.

Match the activities given on the right with the characteristics of the mind on the left.

Note-: There are no right or wrong answers. This exercise is only for you to check your understanding and learning. Each activity can have multiple traits.

	Activity		Characteristic of the mind used
1	Watching your mind for thoughts of anger and irritation without expressing or suppressing them	A	Forcing the mind into present state awareness
2	Sitting in the yogic lotus position in the dark and watching the wick of a candle	B	Starving the mind of attention
3	Playing Dumb Charades	C	Overwhelming the mind with sensory information

	Activity		Characteristic of the mind used
4	Going on a roller coaster ride	D	Confusing the mind with unintelligent input
5	Watching your breath after cooling down after a nail-biting finish of a football match.	E	Focusing the mind on a particular thought or object
6	Meditating in a remote Himalayan village	F	Tricking the mind into survival mode
7	Playing football	G	Using the connection between breath and mind
8	Reading a book on the old Egyptian hieroglyphic script	H	Reducing sensory input to the mind
9	Singing a song at a family gathering	I	Challenging the mind to perform
10	Watching porn	J	Putting the mind under a spotlight

Your Ratings and Review Matter

Now that you have completed reading the book, I ask you kindly to go ahead and give your valuable rating and review.

If this book was useful to you and you were able to learn something new, or you were able to apply some of the techniques successfully, or you liked anything about this book, then my humble request is that you write a review so that it can help and benefit future readers.

I want to change the world through words and communication. I need your help to reach out to as many people as possible.

For an author, there is no greater and better return than a testimonial.

Also, if you want to contact the author or give any kind of feedback, please feel free to write to connect@vishal-gupta.com

Acknowledgments

We cannot do everything ourselves. We all need relatives, friends, and well-wishers, who support us and believe in us.

I thank, from the bottom of my heart, all the people mentioned below for supporting me, believing in me, and for giving their precious time to me so that I could give the best to this book.

THANK YOU!

(Alphabetically) Aalok Mehta, Alka Sooden, Aniket Phule, Anil Agarwal(Dr.), Anoop Pandey, Chetan Bansal, Deepa Shah, Dilip Ahuja, Ibrahim Bohra, Jiya Gupta, Krati Gupta, Prabodh Agarwal, Reena Rupani, Rashmi Agarwal, Saurabh Jain, Samir Agarwal, Satyajit Fovkar, Shashank Shah, Siddhanth Jain, Som Bathla, Sudhanshu Garg, Swati Gupta, Vyom Gupta.

Cover Concept & Design by CREATIVE PLANET : creativeplanetinc@gmail.com

This book is dedicated to
Lord SHIVA
and
Goddess KALI.

I bow down to THEM in
reverence and pay
my respect to their infinite
intelligence and power.

Disclaimer

Although the publisher and the author have made every effort to ensure that the information in this book was correct at press time and while this publication is designed to provide accurate information regarding the subject matter covered, the publisher and the author assume no responsibility for errors, inaccuracies, omissions, or any other inconsistencies herein and hereby disclaim any liability to any party for any loss, damage, or disruption caused by errors or omissions, whether such errors or omissions result from negligence, accident, or any other cause.

The ideas, procedures, and suggestions contained in this book are not intended as a substitute for consulting with an expert.

Neither the author nor the publisher shall be liable or responsible for any loss or damage allegedly arising from any information or suggestion in this book.

Names, characters, and incidents in this book are either the products of the author's imagination or used in a fictitious manner. Any resemblance to an actual person, living or dead, or actual events is purely coincidental.

Copyright © 2020 Vishal Gupta

All rights reserved. No part of this book may be reproduced or transmitted in any form or by any means, electronic or mechanical, without written permission from the author, except for the inclusion of brief quotations in a review. For permission to quote or for bulk orders, please contact the author.

The author can be contacted at:

vishalchief@gmail.com

connect@vishal-gupta.com

Mobile : +91- 9820308218

vishalgupta

Printed in Great Britain
by Amazon

75480956R00068